IAN

EGYPTIAN WARFARE
AND WEAPONS

SHIRE EGYPTOLOGY

2

Cover illustration
Seti I shown charging Libyan enemies: from a nineteenth-century
coloured cast, now at the British Museum, made from a relief
on the north wall of the temple of Amun at Karnak.
(Photograph copyright: Peter Clayton.)

British Library Cataloguing in Publication Data:
Shaw, Ian.
Egyptian warfare and weapons.
I. Title.
932.
ISBN 0-7478-0142-8.

Published by
SHIRE PUBLICATIONS LTD
Cromwell House, Church Street, Princes Risborough,
Buckinghamshire HP17 9AJ, UK.

Series Editor: Barbara Adams.

ISBN 0 7478 0142 8.

First published 1991.

Printed in Great Britain by
C. I. Thomas & Sons (Haverfordwest) Ltd,
Press Buildings, Merlins Bridge, Haverfordwest, Dyfed SA61 1XF.

Contents

Acknowledgements

In writing this book I have received an incalculable amount of encouragement and enthusiasm from Ann Jones, who is also responsible for the line drawings. I am very grateful to Barry Kemp, who read and commented on the final draft of the text, and to Peter Clayton and Kenneth Kitchen, who kindly provided some of the photographs. The dynastic chronology is based on that of Dr William J. Murnane and acknowledgement is made to him and to Penguin Books for its use here.

4

List of illustrations

Chronology

Predynastic Period	*c.*5000-3300 BC		
		5000-4000	Badarian
		4000-3500	Naqada I
		3500-3300	Naqada II
Protodynastic Period	*c.*3300-3050 BC		
Early Dynastic Period	3050-2613 BC		
		3050-2890	Dynasty I
		2890-2686	Dynasty II
		2686-2613	Dynasty III
Old Kingdom	2613-2181 BC		
		2613-2498	Dynasty IV
		2498-2345	Dynasty V
		2345-2181	Dynasty VI

First Intermediate Period	2181-2040 BC	2181-2040	Dynasties VII-X
		2134-2060	Dynasty XI (Theban)
Middle Kingdom	2040-1782 BC	2060-1991	Dynasty XI
		1991-1782	Dynasty XII
Second Intermediate Period	1782-1570 BC	1782-1650	Dynasties XIII-XIV (Egyptian)
		1663-1555	Dynasties XV-XVI (Hyksos)
		1663-1570	Dynasty XVII (Theban)
New Kingdom	1570-1070 BC	1570-1293	Dynasty XVIII
		1570-1546	*Ahmose*
		1504-1450	*Tuthmosis III*
		1386-1349	*Amenophis III*
		1350-1334	*Akhenaten*
		1334-1325	*Tutankhamun*
		1293-1185	Dynasty XIX
		1279-1212	*Ramesses II*
		1185-1070	Dynasty XX
		1182-1151	*Ramesses III*
Third Intermediate Period	1070-713 BC	1070-945	Dynasty XXI
		945-712	Dynasty XXII
		828-712	Dynasty XXIII
		724-713	Dynasty XXIV
Late Period	713-332 BC	713-656	Dynasty XXV (Kushite)
		664-525	Dynasty XXVI (Saite)
		525-404	Dynasty XXVII
		404-399	Dynasty XXVIII
		399-380	Dynasty XXIX
		380-343	Dynasty XXX (Egyptian/Persian)
Graeco-Roman Period	332 BC-AD 395		

1
Introduction

From the great primeval conflict of the gods Horus and Seth to the well documented historical battles at Megiddo and Qadesh, warfare was an essential element in Egyptian culture. If the stereotyped image of Egypt is a nation of priests, scribes and embalmers, the real picture must also include the warriors and generals who maintained the stable conditions within which Egyptian civilisation was able to flourish. The foundations of the pharaonic state itself emerged out of power struggles between the local chiefdoms of the late Predynastic Period.

The vast array of sources for the study of Egyptian warfare is inevitably patchy, particularly in terms of its historical range. For instance, little is known about the organisation of the Egyptian army until the beginning of the second millennium BC, while the primary sources for international diplomacy are restricted to only a few decades in the fourteenth century BC. Overall, however, the flavour and atmosphere of Egyptian army life has been well preserved, whether through paintings of new recruits being given military-style haircuts or in the form of zealously pedantic military dispatches from the Nubian front.

The very fact that the Egyptians retained their independence as a nation for the greater part of three thousand years is evidence enough of their ability to defend their borders and to deal on equal terms with a succession of ancient Near Eastern empires. The fortresses in Nubia and the numerous indications of political intervention in the Levant also indicate that a vigorous policy of expansionism and imperialism was pursued by Egypt for many hundreds of years. The policy was a fundamental part of the Egyptian world view whereby the pharaoh's domains were considered to have originally comprised the whole of creation. Any act of warfare perpetrated by Egypt — whether a punitive raid on a Nubian village or a major expedition into Syria-Palestine — was therefore considered to be a legitimate restoration of the natural order of things.

8   *Egyptian Warfare and Weapons*

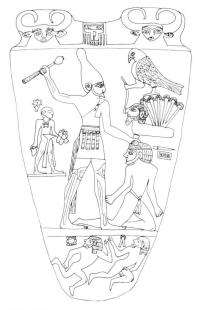 

1. (Above) The Narmer Palette from Hierakonpolis, Protodynastic Period. (Cairo Museum CG 14716.)

2. The Battlefield Palette, showing the Egyptian king in the form of a lion savaging his enemies, probably Libyan invaders, Protodynastic Period. (Ashmolean Museum, Oxford, 1171.1892 [top] and British Museum, EA 20791 [bottom]; reproduced by courtesy of the Trustees of the British Museum.)

2
Egypt's enemies

The earliest depictions of Egyptian kings, such as the Protodynastic Narmer Palette (Cairo, Egyptian Museum, figure 1), employ the motif of the prostrate foreigner as a symbol of Egypt's supremacy over the rest of mankind. In these self-confident icons the Egyptian is portrayed as the norm, conscientiously purging the world of such aberrations as the 'vile Asiatic'. The breaking of a tribal warrior's bow was symbolic of submission, therefore the trampling of the so-called 'Nine Bows' was a vivid embodiment of the king's supremacy over subject peoples (including the Egyptians themselves). The Sphinx Stele of Amenophis II (ruled 1453-1419 BC), in the New Kingdom, provides a graphic verbal description of the Egyptian King dispatching his enemies: 'He bound the heads of the Nine Bows ... He has gathered them all into his fist, his mace has crashed upon their heads ...' The visual image of the king slaughtering foreigners was a crucial and constantly repeated element in Egyptian iconography (figures 2, 5, 19 and 21).

The Egyptians saw the Asiatics and Nubians as the two opposite poles of a hostile world outside the Nile valley; with a typical sense of symmetry, their enemies were sometimes simply referred to as the North and the South. The same air of symmetry is apparent in such objects as the ceremonial cane from the tomb of Tutankhamun (Cairo, Egyptian Museum, figure 3), which is adorned with one head of a Nubian and another of an Asiatic. The iconographic role of Egypt's enemies was so prevalent that it is constantly necessary to distinguish, in the archaeological and textual sources, between purely ritualistic and rhetorical references to foreigners and genuine historical records. Many of the reliefs and statues in Egyptian temples are decorated with rows of captive enemies, often in the form of foreign place-names inscribed within city walls (figure 4).

One important source of information on the specific names of Egypt's enemies is a body of inscriptions known as the Execration Texts, dating from the late Old Kingdom to the reigns of Sesostris III and Amenemhat III (c.1878-1797 BC) of the Middle Kingdom. These texts were lists of hostile forces that the Egyptians wished to destroy — they were written in the hieratic script on small pottery vessels and clay figures of bound captives, which were then deliberately broken and buried. They have been found near tombs at Thebes and Saqqara, and in the so-called 'ritual site' at Mirgissa. The names range from deceased Egyptians to foreign princes and peoples, some of which suggest a detailed knowledge of the places and peoples of Nubia and Syria-Palestine. It is clear,

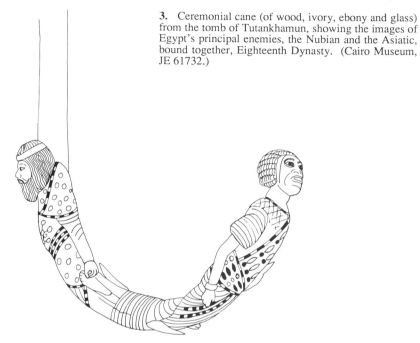

3. Ceremonial cane (of wood, ivory, ebony and glass) from the tomb of Tutankhamun, showing the images of Egypt's principal enemies, the Nubian and the Asiatic, bound together, Eighteenth Dynasty. (Cairo Museum, JE 61732.)

however, that lists of old and new enemies were often mixed together, transforming the Execration Texts into powerful universal statements. The sentiments of the Texts are, however, in direct contrast with the Egyptians' apparently relaxed attitudes to the immigration of foreigners into their society.

For most of the Dynastic Period the Nubians (or Nehesyw) were the inevitable underdogs of the Egyptian system, constantly 'crushed', 'vile' and 'wretched'. From the First Dynasty onwards, military campaigns and trading expeditions were sent into Nubia at regular intervals, providing a steady supply of prisoners, herds of cattle and exotic products from the south such as ivory, ostrich feathers and ebony. The inscriptions in the tombs of the nobles at Elephantine, in Egypt's southernmost province, refer to numerous forays against the Nubians.

By the early New Kingdom the conquest of Nubia was so complete that the whole territory from Aswan to Napata was placed under the command of a viceroy known as 'King's Son of Kush' — Nubia had effectively become a province of Egypt. The icon of the Nubian as defeated enemy, however, never lost its popularity as a symbol of Egyptian success. The official view of the Nubians is exemplified by a

Middle Kingdom boundary stele of Sesostris III from Semna (Berlin, Ägyptisches Museum) which denounces them as follows:

'They are not people one respects; they are wretches, craven-hearted. My majesty has seen it, it is not an untruth. I have captured their women, I have carried off their dependents ...' (Lichtheim, 1973: 119).

It is ironic that, even in the Meroitic Period, when Nubian rulers had inherited the Egyptian pharaohs' mantle, the same traditional motifs of the defeated Nubian were still depicted in the royal regalia, with no apparent sense of contradiction.

The Libyans (known as the Tjehenu or Tjemehu) occupied the lands to the north-west of the Nile valley and were portrayed by the Egyptians as dark-skinned, bearded (and occasionally fair-haired and blue-eyed), semi-nomadic peoples. The Protodynastic ceremonial palettes and the temple reliefs of the Dynastic Period frequently show them as defeated enemies (figures 2 and 5), and there are records from the reigns of the Old Kingdom pharaohs Sneferu and Sahure of specific campaigns against the Libyans.

4. Line of foreign captives with their bodies in the form of walled towns containing the names of peoples and places, such as Shasu (the Bedouin), second from left. Relief from the northern side of the outer wall of the Ptolemaic temple of Kom Ombo. (Photograph: Ian Shaw.)

5. Figure of Ramesses III smiting a Libyan on the southern wall of the temple of Medinet Habu, Twentieth Dynasty. (Photograph: Ian Shaw.)

The reliefs in two mortuary temples of the Old Kingdom (those of Sahure at Abusir and Pepi II at Saqqara), as well as the Late Period temple of Taharqa at Kawa, include the stock scene of a Libyan chieftain being slaughtered by the king while his wife and children beg for mercy. The repetition of the same personal names for the Libyans in all three scenes suggests that they were part of the elaborate ritual of kingship rather than records of actual historical events. It is clear, however, that the Egyptians were obliged to undertake periodic punitive campaigns against the Libyans throughout the Dynastic Period. Eventually, in the New Kingdom, Merneptah (ruled 1212-1202 BC) and Ramesses III (ruled 1182-1151 BC) were obliged to stave off a major invasion from Libya. In the late New Kingdom Libyans and other foreign prisoners were often settled in military colonies within Egypt. These resettled Libyans, known as Meshwesh, became an influential group in Egyptian society and eventually gained temporary control of the country in the Twenty-second Dynasty (*c*.945-712 BC).

Beyond the north-eastern border of Egypt, across the Sinai peninsula, were the various peoples of Syria-Palestine. A distinction must be made between the simple iconographic image of the bound and enslaved Asiatic and the more complex reality of the economic and political links, whereby Egyptians obtained goods from the Levant, particularly the timber which was so scarce in Egypt. In the Instruction to King Merikare, a didactic text dating originally to the First Intermediate Period, the scribe's description of the typical Asiatic suggests a growing familiarity with the geography of Syria-Palestine: 'Lo, the miserable Asiatic, he is wretched because of the place he is in: short of water, bare of wood, its paths are many and painful because of mountains' (Lichtheim, 1973: 103-4).

During the Old and Middle Kingdoms there seem to have been relatively few Egyptian military campaigns of any significance in Western Asia. In the Second Intermediate Period Egypt itself was ruled by a dynasty of Asiatic kings known as the Hyksos, 'rulers of foreign lands'. The eventual expulsion of the Hyksos by King Ahmose developed inexorably into an aggressive policy of imperialism in Syria-Palestine, which was eventually to bring the New Kingdom pharaohs into direct confrontation with the great powers beyond the Levant: Mitanni, Hatti (the Kingdom of the Hittites) and Assyria.

6. View of the *migdol* gateway at Medinet Habu, Twentieth Dynasty. (Photograph: Ian Shaw.)

3
Fortresses and frontiers

Symbolism and functions of Egyptian fortifications

To some extent all Egyptian ceremonial buildings, including temples and funerary complexes, were intended to function as bastions of order and harmony, requiring at least symbolic fortifications to protect them from the surrounding chaos. Medinet Habu, the mortuary temple of the Twentieth Dynasty king Ramesses III at Thebes, was surrounded by a fortified enclosure wall with two gateways imitating contemporary Syrian fortresses or *migdols*, complete with crenellated battlements (figure 6). It is clear that the whole complex was at once both a religious centre and a monument to Ramesses III's military prowess. Conversely, the distinctive features of Egyptian forts, with their symmetrical and often elegant designs, probably reflect the monumental traditions of Egyptian religious architecture just as much as pragmatic military requirements.

The earliest surviving Egyptian fortifications were built to protect towns rather than to defend frontiers. Apart from the hieroglyphic symbols for 'city' (*niwt*) and 'enclosure' (*ḥwt*), which are plans of circular and rectangular enclosure walls (figure 7), a number of detailed representations of fortified towns have survived from the earliest times in Egypt (see figure 1). Probably the first evidence for an Egyptian fortress is a Predynastic ceramic model of a building, discovered by Flinders Petrie at Abadiyeh, which appears to show two men peering over a crenellated wall (Oxford, Ashmolean Museum; figure 8). Memphis, the capital of Egypt for most of its history, was said to have been founded in the form of a fortress called the White Wall by Menes, the first king of Egypt.

The paintings in the tombs of two Eleventh Dynasty provincial governors, Khety (number 17, figure 9) and Baqt III (number 15), at Beni Hasan, include depictions of soldiers laying siege to fortified towns in Egypt during the civil wars of the late First Intermediate Period. These fortifications appear to have consisted of high walls, crenellated at the top and strengthened with a slight batter at the base. The numerous wounds found on the heads of sixty Eleventh Dynasty soldiers (buried in a mass grave near the tomb of Nebhepetre Mentuhotep II at Deir el-Bahri) probably bear witness to the fatal consequences of attempting to storm such battlements.

The defence of Egypt's frontiers

The question of Egyptian fortresses, as opposed to fortified towns, is very closely connected with that of frontiers. The traditional borders of

7. Hieroglyphic symbols for fortifications: (left to right) *niwt*, *ḥwt* and *'ḥ*.

Egypt comprised the Western Desert, the Sinai Desert, the Mediterranean coast and the First Nile Cataract at Aswan. Such natural physical barriers were sufficient to protect the Egyptians from outside interference for the many centuries during which their distinctive civilisation developed. Later on in the Dynastic Period these natural borders helped to maintain Egypt's independence during periods of relative weakness. Since, however, the pharaoh's title described him as the ruler of the entire known world, the political boundaries of Egypt were theoretically infinite. In times of strength and prosperity certain rulers, such as Sesostris I and Tuthmosis III, declared their intention to 'extend the borders' of Egypt. In practice the furthest extent of the Egyptian empire — achieved during the reign of Tuthmosis III in the Eighteenth Dynasty — was marked by the Euphrates in the north-east and the Kurgus boundary stele (between the Fourth and Fifth Nile Cataracts) in the south. The north-eastern, north-western and southern borders of Egypt were more or less fortified from the the time of the Middle Kingdom onwards.

From at least the reign of Amenemhat I (ruled 1991-1962 BC) the eastern Delta was protected by a string of fortresses, known as the

8. Clay model of battlements from Abadiyeh, Predynastic Period. (Ashmolean Museum, Oxford, E.3202; reproduced by courtesy of the Visitors of the Ashmolean Museum, Oxford.)

9. Scene of siege warfare showing the use of a battering ram, from the tomb of Khety at Beni Hasan, Middle Kingdom.

Walls of the Prince. These were intended to prevent invasion along the coastal route from the Levant, which was known as the Way of Horus during the Middle Kingdom. At about the same time a fortress seems to have been established in the Wadi Natrun, defending the western Delta from the Libyans. The western and eastern Delta defences were well maintained throughout the second millennium BC. The New Kingdom fortresses and garrisons of the Delta borders — including el-Alamein and Zawiyet Umm el-Rakham in the west and Tell Abu Safa (Sile), Tell el-Farama (Pelusium), Tell el-Heir (Migdol) and Tell el-Maskhuta (Pithom) in the east — were intended to prevent any recurrence of the ignominious imposition of foreign rule by the Hyksos dynasty.

In the south of Egypt, the border with Kush (Lower Nubia) was traditionally marked by the town of Elephantine, naturally defended by its island location and surrounded by a thick defensive wall. The original name of the settlement around the First Cataract was Swn, meaning 'trade' (from which the modern name Aswan derives); this place-name reflects the more commercial nature of the southern border, representing opportunities for profitable economic activities rather than the threat of invasion. Because the First Cataract constituted an obstacle to shipping (despite an attempt by the Old Kingdom ruler Merenre to cut a canal), all trade goods had to be transported along the bank. This crucial land route to the east of the Nile, between Aswan and the region of Philae, was protected by a huge mud-brick wall, almost 7.5 km ($4^{1}/_{2}$ miles) long, probably built principally in the Twelfth Dynasty. The land route at the Second Cataract (in the region of Semna) was defended by a similar fortification.

The Nubian fortresses

In the Old Kingdom (*c*.2613-2181 BC) the Egyptian presence in Nubia seems to have principally consisted of a succession of trading and mining expeditions, peacefully exploiting valuable animal and mineral resources. Probably the earliest surviving permanently occupied Egyptian outpost in Nubia was a small Old Kingdom settlement at Buhen near the Second Cataract, which was protected by a large, crudely built stone wall. This site has been dated to the Fourth and Fifth Dynasties (and possibly as early as the Second Dynasty) and was apparently devoted primarily to the smelting of copper. During the Middle Kingdom, however, the Egyptians embarked on a programme of military expansion into Nubia, bolstering their position with a long chain of fortresses between modern Aswan and the region of the Second Cataract (see figure 10). These heavily fortified settlements, located at the most vulnerable points in the trade route from the south, were simultaneously both military outposts and customs stations. Most of them have now vanished irretrievably beneath the waters of Lake Nasser since the raising of the Aswan High Dam in 1971. Fortunately, however, the rescue excavations of the Nubian Salvage Campaign (1959-69) have provided a great deal of information concerning this unique group of sites.

Virtually all of the forts were built, mainly in mud brick, over a period of 130 years (*c*.1971-1841 BC), from the reign of Sesostris I to that of his great-grandson Sesostris III. A large cluster of eleven fortresses was established by Sesostris III in the area of the Second Cataract, each positioned in order to control the flow of traffic northwards at points where the Nile was difficult to negotiate. The southernmost of these (Semna, Kumma, Uronarti and Semna South) were located about 50 km (30 miles) south of the Second Cataract, around the narrowest gorge in the whole course of the Nile, marking the final frontier in the Twelfth Dynasty. The role of these forts is clarified by the text of a stele set up by Sesostris III at Semna:

'Southern boundary, made in the year 8, under the majesty of the King of Upper and Lower Egypt, Khakaura Sesostris III who is given life forever and ever; in order to prevent that any negro should cross it, by water or by land, with a ship, or any herds of the negroes; except a negro who shall come to do trading in Iken [Mirgissa] or with a commission. Every good thing shall be done with them, but without allowing a ship of the negroes to pass by Heh [Semna?], going downstream, forever.'

The main reason for the Second Cataract forts was evidently not the protection of Egypt's southern border, for they would have been easily outflanked by invaders passing along the desert on either side. Nor

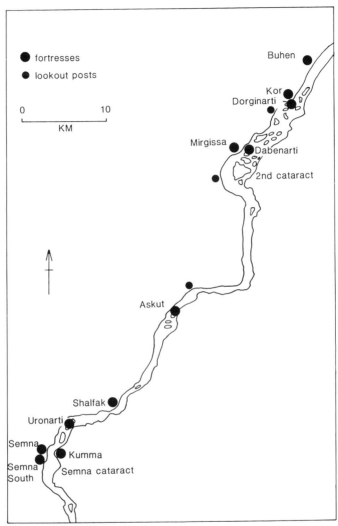

10. Map of the Second Cataract fortresses in Nubia, from Buhen to Semna South, Middle Kingdom. (After Adams.)

● fortresses

● lookout posts

0 _____ 10

KM

Buhen

Kor
Dorginarti

Mirgissa
Dabenarti

2nd cataract

Askut

Shalfak

Uronarti

Semna

Semna
South

Kumma

Semna cataract

were the forts simply designed to subjugate Lower Nubia, since the local population does not seem to have been considered a great threat and the names of the Middle Kingdom forts appear to refer to enemies located further south (perhaps because they provided bases from which to launch attacks on Upper Nubia). They seem to have functioned primarily as a means of enforcing the Egyptian king's monopoly on trade goods (especially gold, ivory, animals and slaves) emanating from African peoples further to the south, through Upper Nubia, which was known to the Egyptians of the Old Kingdom as Yam.

11. View of the north-west ramparts at Buhen, Middle Kingdom. (Reproduced by courtesy of the Egypt Exploration Society.)

By the New Kingdom (and perhaps earlier) the Second Cataract forts were united under the command of Buhen, the traditional centre of Egyptian operations in Nubia (figure 11). A series of lookout posts, consisting of clusters of rough stone huts (often accompanied by graffiti carved in the cliff face) at strategic high points along the banks, helped to maintain strong communication links between the forts. A set of dispatches from the Semna fortress (London, BM, EA 10752; see chapter 4) contains evidence of the close watch kept on the movements of foreigners in the vicinity of the Second Cataract. All information, however trivial, was conveyed back to the military headquarters in Thebes. Another Papyrus — the so-called Ramesseum Onomasticon (Papyrus Berlin 10495) — lists the bellicose names of seventeen of the Nubian forts, including 'Repelling the Seti', 'Warding off the Bows' and 'Curbing the Countries'.

All of the Second Cataract forts had similar internal plans, consisting of a grid plan of specialised zones for storerooms, workshops, barracks and officers' houses. These various quarters were linked and intersected by a network of well constructed streets and drains, often built of stone. The whole community was usually encircled by a street around the inside of the walls (known as a *pomoerium*), allowing troops speedy and convenient access to the battlements. Most of the forts were linked with the Nile by covered or walled stairways. The Semna South fortress was provided with a granite-lined tunnel, passing under the riverside defences, which appears to have been intended to provide an alternative supply of fresh water, presumably in the event of a siege.

Although the general uniformity of the Middle Kingdom forts' ground plans suggests that they were probably designed by only one or two architects, they show fascinating variations in response to the local topography (see figure 12). Whereas the two largest sites, Buhen and Mirgissa, were simply rectangular structures (as were all five of the surviving forts north of the Second Cataract group), the rest had idiosyncratic shapes dictated by the terrain. The fort at Semna, for instance, was built in an L shape in order to conform with the rocky hill on which it stood. At Uronarti, an island near Semna, the fort was triangular in shape and the northern side was more heavily fortified with huge

12. Plans of the Egyptian fortresses at A, Semna; B, Uronarti; C, Shalfak; and D, Buhen. (After Adams.)

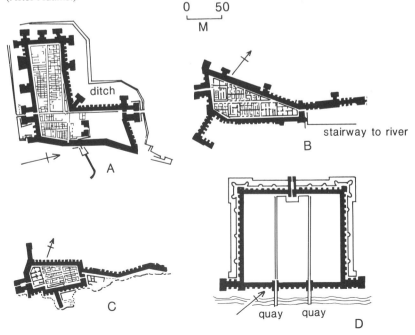

towers, since the flatter terrain to the north made attacks from that direction more dangerous. In addition two long spur walls stretched away from the main Uronarti fort to the south and north-east, so that the whole irregular island was afforded maximum protection. Spur walls were used in the same way at Shalfak and Askut.

By far the most elaborate of the Nubian fortresses were Mirgissa, Buhen and Aniba. Mirgissa, now securely identified with the fort named as Iken in Sesostris III's Semna stele, consisted of a whole complex of smaller sites, including the fortress itself, two separate towns (only one of which was fortified), two cemeteries, a ditch filled with statues and pottery bearing Execration Texts, and the small, apparently unfinished island fortress of Dabenarti. As at Uronarti, one side of the main Mirgissa fortress (facing the Western Desert) was felt to be more vulnerable to attack and was therefore given an additional outer wall. Inside the fort the excavations revealed an armoury of spears, arrows and shields at various stages in the manufacturing process (see figure 26).

Buhen was located at the northern end of the Second Cataract region, so that the Nile was from then on easily navigable up to the First Cataract at Aswan. It was well situated to act as a large depot for trade goods from the Middle Kingdom until the late New Kingdom. The grandiose defences included an outer enclosure wall over 700 metres long and 4 metres thick. The wall was strengthened at intervals by 32 semicircular bastions; this outer defence was probably intended to protect the builders while the complicated inner fortifications were being constructed. The western wall had five large towers as well as a huge central tower which functioned as the main gateway to the site; this entrance (known as the Barbican) was gradually strengthened over the years, developing into a huge tower, measuring 47 by 30 metres, with two baffle entrances, double wooden doors and even a drawbridge on rollers. The inner walls of the fort, 5 metres thick and at least 11 metres high, also had square towers at the corners and bastions at 5 metre intervals, each provided with triple loop-holes through which archers could fire on attackers. Both outer and inner defences were surrounded by ditches following the outline of the walls, with salients at the points where towers or bastions projected from the outer surface. Although Buhen was undoubtedly the most sophisticated Middle Kingdom fortress in Nubia, most of its elements — such as loopholes, berms, counterscarps, glacis and bastions — also appear to varying degrees in the other contemporary forts.

The roles of the fortresses further north in Lower Nubia seem to have been more idiosyncratic. Aniba must have originally had some connections with the diorite quarries about 80 km (50 miles) to the south-west, but since it was located amid an area of relatively dense Nubian population it may have been the only Middle Kingdom garrison specifically intended as a military check on the Lower Nubians themselves. The northernmost fort, Kubban, 100 km (60 miles) south of Aswan, was perhaps founded as early as the Old Kingdom; it was evidently intended to protect the Egyptian copper and gold mining expeditions in the Wadi Allaqi. The purpose of the forts at Faras and Serra, only about 15-25 km (10-15 miles) north of Buhen, is not clear, since they appear to be associated neither with crucial trading points nor with centres of population (although the inclusion of part of the river within the defences at Serra perhaps suggests a concern with regulation of river traffic). The Faras and Serra forts provide strong support for the argument that, in the last resort, the Middle Kingdom Nubian fortresses were primarily architectural propaganda: bombastic displays of the Twelfth Dynasty's obsession with order and domination.

The purely symbolic aspect of the Nubian fortifications became even more of a factor in the New Kingdom, during which a more sophisticated foreign policy was developed. The original Middle Kingdom fortifications were repaired and sometimes even elaborated (partly in response to such technological innovations as chariotry), but the settlements themselves became more like towns than garrisons; magnificent stone temples began to be built both inside and outside the bounds of the towers and bastions. New towns were established at such sites as Sesebi, Soleb, Aksha and Amara West. Although these New Kingdom towns were located further south than the Second Cataract forts, their defences were perfunctory, usually comprising a single mud-brick wall with towers at intervals, unprotected by the complex ditches and glacis of the Middle Kingdom forts. The Egyptians of the New Kingdom obviously felt sufficiently confident of their control of Nubia to transfer their resources from fortifications to temples.

In the troubled times of the Third Intermediate Period and Late Period (see chapter 8) there was a renewed proliferation of fortifications. The stele of the Kushite King Piye at Gebel Barkal (figure 50), describing his victory over the Egyptians in 734 BC, mentions nineteen fortified settlements in Middle Egypt as well as 'walled cities' in the Delta region. Piye's own invasion of Egypt involved laying siege both to Hermopolis Magna and to Memphis, as the Egyptian armies were driven further northward.

Massive forts and walls continued to be built in Egypt — from Ramesses II's string of forts along the Mediterranean coast of the Delta to the Roman forts at Qasr Ibrim and Qasr Qarun (Dionysias) — but the sheer ambition and technical precocity of the Second Cataract fortifications remained unparalleled.

13. (Left) Wooden military ration tokens from the fortress of Uronarti, Middle Kingdom. (Museum of Fine Arts, Boston, A3319; reproduced by courtesy of Museum of Fine Arts, Boston.)

14. (Below) Papyrus bearing the hieratic text of one of the 'Semna Dispatches', Middle Kingdom. (British Museum, EA 10752; reproduced by courtesy of the Trustees of the British Museum.)

4
The Egyptian army

The Old Kingdom

Evidence concerning the composition and organisation of the Egyptian army has survived primarily in the form of detailed battle descriptions on the walls of temples and lists of titles on the walls of soldiers' tombs. At first, in the Old Kingdom, the militaristic element in Egyptian society was clearly not as powerful as the forces of bureaucracy and the priesthood. Since there was apparently no need for a permanent standing army (apart from a small royal bodyguard), armies of young men were periodically conscripted on a relatively *ad hoc* basis for a variety of labour-intensive purposes from quarrying and trading expeditions to military campaigns and the policing of civil disturbances.

The autobiography of a noble called Weni, at Abydos, describes the large-scale conscription of men from Egypt and Nubia for a campaign in Palestine during the reign of Pepi I (ruled 2332-2283 BC). The 'many tens of thousands' of soldiers in Weni's army were made up of various local corps supplied by provincial officials. There does not appear to have been any overall military hierarchy or organisation in the Old Kingdom, although the title 'overseer of soldiers' was occasionally used, and the fortresses on Egypt's borders were controlled by the 'overseer of desert blockhouses and royal fortresses'. *Tst* (a term roughly corresponding to 'battalion') was the only word used to describe units of soldiers in the Old Kingdom. The political history of Egypt in the Old Kingdom was marked by the gradual devolution of power to the provinces, so that by the First Intermediate Period each local governor was entitled to recruit his own private army (see figure 22).

The Middle Kingdom

The first indications of a more ambitious and systematic approach to military organisation are to be found in the Nubian policy of Amenemhat I (ruled 1991-1962 BC) and his successors. The campaigns of the royal army in Nubia were initially reinforced by provincial governors' troops. By the reign of Sesostris III, however, the power of the governors had been greatly reduced, perhaps partly as a result of the existence of a more professional and highly organised royal army in Nubia. The establishment of a string of fortresses to control Nubia (see chapter 3) necessitated the deployment of permanent garrisons of soldiers and a complex network of command. The excavations of the Nubian fortresses have provided a great deal of evidence concerning the day-to-day maintenance of the garrisons. At Uronarti, for instance, wooden tallies in the shapes of different loaves were apparently issued to the soldiers for use as bread-ration tokens, each corresponding to a number of loaves such as sixty or ninety (figure 13).

Further information concerning Middle Kingdom military organisation in Nubia has come from a cache of papyri discovered by James Quibell in a tomb shaft under the granaries of the mortuary temple of Ramesses II at Thebes. Among these texts, now in the British Museum, were the Ramesseum Ononasticon and the so-called Semna Dispatches, a set of hieratic communiqués between the forts in Nubia (EA 10752, figure 14), probably sent in the third year of Amenemhat III's reign (c.1841 BC). The messages deal with the close military surveillance of the regions around the forts, as in the case of one communication sent from the guard Ameny (at the Serra East fort) to a commander in the Theban administration:

> 'It is a communication to the Master, may he live prosper and be healthy, to the effect that the soldier of Nekhen ... came to report this to your servant at breakfast time on the 2nd day of the 4th month of spring, in the 3rd year, on a mission from the officer of the town regiment, Khusobek's son Mentuhotep's son, Khusobek ... who is acting in lieu of the officer of the sovereign's crew in the garrison of Meha (a district of Nubia), saying: "The patrol that went out to patrol the desert-edge near the fortress of Khesef-Medjau [Serra East] on the last day of the 3rd month of spring in the 3rd year has returned to report to me, saying: We have found the track of 32 men and 3 donkeys ..." '

Two principal elements of Middle Kingdom military organisation are readily apparent in this letter: the transference to the army of the Egyptian bureaucrats' precise attention to detail and the existence of a complex chain of command from commander down to infantryman.

Nubia was necessarily heavily militarised in the Middle Kingdom, but in Egypt itself the influence of soldiers seems to have been less overt. By the late Middle Kingdom, however, there were a number of precise military titles in use in Egypt, including 'head commander of the town regiment', 'soldier of the town regiment', 'commander of the leaders of dog patrols' and 'scribe of the army'.

The New Kingdom

In the early Eighteenth Dynasty the pressing demands of Egyptian imperialism led to the establishment of a large professional army, the hierarchy of which (figure 15) also provided an alternative route to power, particularly for the uneducated. The traditional scribally trained clerical administrators learned to share power with the new military class that was to play an important role in the rise of the warrior pharaohs of the Eighteenth to Twentieth Dynasties.

Within Egypt itself there were evidently two basic corps of the army, corresponding to the north and south of the country, according to an edict issued by Horemheb. Troops of provincial soldiers served ten-

MILITARY ORGANISATION

Types of troops:
infantry
chariotry
garrison/outpost
élite troops
ship contingent
foreign troops

Sizes of units:
army division = *c*.5000
host = 500+ (at least 2 companies)
company = 250 (5 platoons)
platoon = 50 (5 squads)
squad = 10

Hierarchy:

KING
|
COMMANDER-IN-CHIEF
[usually king's son]

CHIEF DEPUTY   CHIEF DEPUTY
OF THE NORTHERN CORPS   OF THE SOUTHERN CORPS

GENERAL
|
SCRIBE OF INFANTRY
|
COMMANDER OF A HOST
|
STANDARD-BEARER
|
ADJUTANT/DEPUTY

Scribal administration   Combat officers

DISTRIBUTION SCRIBE   PLATOON LEADER
| |
ASSEMBLAGE SCRIBE   GARRISON-TROOP LEADER
| |
ARMY SCRIBE   SQUAD LEADER
|
INFANTRYMAN

15. Chart showing the organisation and hierarchy of the Egyptian armed forces in the New Kingdom.

16. Scene of five Nubian mercenaries, one carrying a military standard, from the tomb of Tjanuny at Thebes, New Kingdom.

day shifts as members of the royal bodyguard. In terms of campaigning, on the other hand, there were three or four principal divisions of the Egyptian army, each numbering about five thousand soldiers, consisting of a combination of conscripts and professionals. According to various inscriptions of Seti I and Ramesses II, these divisions were each given the name of a god followed by an epithet, such as 'Amun, Rich of Bows' or 'Pre, Numerous of Heroes'. It has been suggested that the gods in question were probably the local deities of the regions from which the recruits had been enlisted. Each division was commanded by a general, literally the 'great overseer of the division', a post dating back to the Middle Kingdom, who was invariably one of the king's sons.

For tactical purposes, the basic military unit was the platoon of fifty infantrymen, each under the command of a 'chief of fifty'. There were usually five platoons in a 'company' and about twenty companies in a division (see figure 15). The units of infantrymen were reinforced by separate companies of 'élite troops' and 'chariot warriors'. It appears that the officers in charge of units of chariot warriors were frequently promoted to prestigious diplomatic posts such as 'royal envoy'. As well as the hierarchy of purely military officials there was also a separate, superimposed chain of command made up of officials drawn from the civil administration (such as scribes, quartermasters, adjutants and stablemasters). Judging from the accounts of the battles of Megiddo and Qadesh (see chapter 6), the overall tactics and campaign strategies were dictated by a council made up of the king and his generals.

Training and active service

The instruction of New Kingdom soldiers, which took place in special military training camps, seems to have involved a combination of drill practice and regular physical punishment. The decoration in the Theban tomb of Userhat (TT 56), an army officer at the time of Amenophis II, includes scenes of the reception of recruits, barbers cutting soldiers' hair, and quartermasters issuing rations. The tomb of Tjanuny (TT 74), an army scribe in the reign of Tuthmosis IV, contains similar scenes, including a magnificent depiction of five marching Nubian mercenaries wearing long net-like kilts reinforced with leather and decorated with leopards' tails (figure 16). One carries a military standard — a constant feature of Egyptian warfare since Protodynastic times — bearing a depiction of two wrestlers. Another scene in Tjanuny's tomb shows well fed cattle being herded into the army camp as food for the troops.

Among Ramesses II's reliefs of the battle of Qadesh there are two (on the west wing of the Luxor temple pylon and on the north wall of the Great Temple at Abu Simbel) that include detailed depictions of the temporary camp set up by the Egyptian army on the move. The encamped soldiery, as well as stables for horses and cattle, are shown surrounded by a rectangular barricade of shields. In the centre of the camp was the royal pavilion, surrounded by the smaller rectangular-framed tents of the military hierarchy.

These images present a vivid and relatively congenial view of army life, whereas many of the literary texts of New Kingdom scribes were obviously designed to discourage the young from pursuing a military career. Papyrus Anastasi III presents a typically jaundiced outlook on army life:

'Come, I will describe to you the lot of the infantryman, the much exerted one: he is brought as a child of *nbi* and confined to a barrack. A painful blow is dealt to his body, a savage blow to his eye and a splitting blow to his brow. His head is split open with a wound. He is laid down and beaten like a piece of papyrus. He is lambasted with beatings. Come, I will describe to you his journey to the land of Kharu and his march over the hills: his bread and water are carried on his shoulders like a donkey's burden. His neck becomes calloused, like a donkey's, and the arches of his back are bent. He drinks foul-tasting water and halts to stand guard. When he reaches the enemy he is like a pinioned bird, with no strength in his limbs. If he succeeds in returning to Egypt he is like a stick that the woodworm has eaten — he is full of sickness. He is carried back in a state of paralysis on the back of a donkey. His clothes have been stolen and his retainer has run away.'

Certainly the Egyptian soldier would have undergone enormous physical suffering both in training and in action, but the rich rewards of survival — in the form of personal advancement, spoils of war and gifts of land and livestock upon retirement from military service — must have helped to compensate for this. The Wilbour Papyrus, a list of people renting land in Middle Egypt during the fourth year of the reign of Ramesses V (*c*.1142 BC), includes many veteran soldiers, such as Sherden mercenaries.

Mercenaries

From the Early Dynastic Period the Egyptian army had frequently included Nubian mercenaries. The Medjay, a nomadic group originally from the eastern deserts of Nubia, were commonly employed as scouts and light infantry from the Second Intermediate Period onwards. They have been identified with the archaeological remains of the so-called Pan-grave people, who eventually appear to have been absorbed into the Egyptian population. By the time of Amenophis III, soldiers of many different nationalities (Syrian, Libyan, Sherden, Shekelesh and even Hittites) had begun to be drafted into the Egyptian ranks, often in the form of branded prisoners permitted to win their freedom by taking up arms on behalf of Egypt. A painted limestone stele from Amarna (Berlin, Ägyptisches Museum) shows a Syrian mercenary in an elaborate kilt apparently relaxing with his wife, while an Egyptian servant helps him drink from a jug through a type of reed straw (figure 17).

17. A Syrian mercenary and his wife, depicted on a stele found at Amarna, New Kingdom. (Ägyptisches Museum, Berlin.)

5
Weapons and military technology

Predynastic weaponry

The principal weapons in the late Predynastic and Protodynastic Periods were undoubtedly the bow and arrow, spear, axe and mace. These are frequently shown in relief depictions of hunting and battle scenes (figure 18). Comparatively large numbers of maceheads have been excavated at late Predynastic and Protodynastic sites. The mace was the simplest of weapons, consisting of a stone head attached to a wooden haft, often tapering towards the end that was gripped. At first the most common form of macehead was disc-shaped, but this was gradually replaced by a pear-shaped type, which usually had a longer haft. In the battles that led to the unification of Egypt the mace seems to have played an important role in general hand-to-hand fighting. One of the scenes in the so-called Painted Tomb at Hierakonpolis (dating to the Naqada II period; c.3500-3300 BC) shows a warrior — perhaps a king or prince — apparently threatening a row of prisoners with a mace (figure 19).

By the Protodynastic Period the actual surface of the macehead, like the ceremonial cosmetic palette, had been adopted as a vehicle for royal propaganda. The limestone maceheads of Scorpion (see figure 20) and Narmer, for instance, both excavated from the so-called Main Deposit of the temple at Hierakonpolis, and both now in the Ashmolean Museum, Oxford, were decorated with scenes illustrating important religious and political events. A scene on the Narmer Palette (Cairo, Egyptian Museum), showing King Narmer dispatching a kneeling captive with a ceremonial mace, is the first clear instance of the transformation of the mace into a primary symbol of royal domination rather than a simple weapon. The walls of Graeco-Roman temples continued to depict Pharaoh in the act of smiting foreigners with a mace long after the weapon itself had fallen out of general use (figure 21).

The throwstick or boomerang (a curved wooden blade) was also a traditional Egyptian weapon dating back to Predynastic times. Although it continued in use as a weapon during the Dynastic Period (some of Queen Hatshepsut's soldiers on a trading mission to Punt, for instance, appear to have been armed with throwsticks), its primary use was in the hunting of birds.

The conservatism of the armoury

In the Dynastic Period it is the sheer uniformity and lack of change in Egyptian weaponry that is most striking, considering the military power

18. Detail of the Hunter's Palette, showing three Early Dynastic warriors carrying various weapons, including a throwstick, a mace and a bow and arrow. (British Museum, EA 20790.)

achieved by the Egyptian empire at its peak. There was a gradual improvement in the military hardware available to Egyptian soldiers, but the principal changes did not take place until the beginning of the New Kingdom. After the Early Dynastic Period Egyptian arms remained similar to those in use in Africa and Palestine — suggesting that territorial gains in the Old and Middle Kingdoms must have owed more to superior organisation than to military technology.

The soldiers of the Old and Middle Kingdoms wore no armour. In the Old Kingdom they are usually depicted wearing only a belt and a small triangular loincloth, and by the Middle Kingdom their costume was invariably the same short linen kilt as that worn by civilian workmen. The mass grave of sixty Theban soldiers from the reign of Nebhepetre Mentuhotep II contained numerous textiles, including fringed kilts, some apparently bearing official laundry marks.

From the late Predynastic Period to the Middle Kingdom, Egyptian soldiers' only bodily protection (apart from the occasional use of a band

19. Detail of the painting in the Hierakonpolis Painted Tomb, showing a warrior threatening a row of prisoners with a mace, late Predynastic Period. (After Kemp 1989.)

20. (Right) The lime-
stone 'Scorpion' mace-
head from Hierakon-
polis, Protodynastic
Period. (Ashmolean
Museum, Oxford,
E.3632; reproduced by
courtesy of the Visitors
of the Ashmolean
Museum, Oxford.)

21. (Below) Scene of
the Roman emperor
Trajan smiting foreign-
ers in the presence of
the ram-god Khnum,
on the exterior of the
north wall of the tem-
ple of Khnum at Esna,
Graeco-Roman Period.
(Photograph: Ian
Shaw.)

22. Painted wooden model of Egyptian soldiers from the tomb of Mesehti at Asyut, Middle Kingdom. (Cairo Museum, JE 30986; reproduced by courtesy of Peter Clayton.)

of webbing across the shoulders and chest) was supplied by long, roughly rectangular shields made of cowhide stretched over a wooden frame. They were either 1 metre or 1.5 metres high and usually tapered towards the top to a curved or pointed edge. Handles for gripping were carved out of the middle of the wooden framework. Leather straps could also be attached to the handle for occasions (such as siege warfare) when the shield needed to be carried across the shoulder, leaving both hands free.

One of the most important sources for the study of Egyptian weapons in the early Middle Kingdom is a pair of painted wooden models (Cairo, Egyptian Museum) from the tomb of Mesehti, a provincial governor at Asyut in the Eleventh Dynasty (figure 22). Forty Egyptian spearmen and forty Nubian archers are reproduced in faithful detail, showing the typical costume and arms of the common soldier. The Egyptian spearmen are wearing short linen kilts and carry a shield in the left hand and a spear, with a long leaf-shaped bronze blade, in the right. Each shield is painted with a different design imitating the mottled markings of cowhide. The Nubian archers are dressed somewhat differently, in more elaborate green and red loincloths, probably made from leather rather than linen. They carry their wooden recurved bows in one hand and bunches of arrows in the other. Another tomb at Asyut, belonging to a Twelfth Dynasty nobleman called Nakht, was found to contain a whole replica armoury, including full-size spears (of a very similar type to those in Mesehti's model), two cylindrical spear-cases, two bows and arrows and a shield (Cairo, Egyptian Museum, and Paris, Louvre).

Throughout the Dynastic Period one of the most commonly used

23. (Right) The development of the Egyptian battleaxe: A, semicircular axehead (Old and Middle Kingdoms); B, long axehead (Middle Kingdom); C, 'scalloped' or 'tanged' axehead (Middle Kingdom); D, long narrow axehead (New Kingdom); E, openwork axehead (New Kingdom).

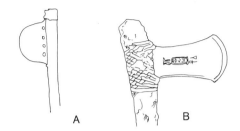

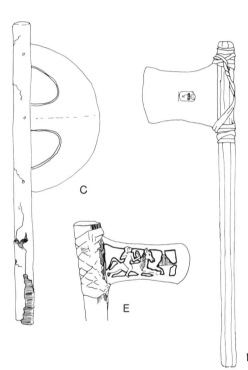

A

B

C

E

D

24. (Below) Middle Kingdom battleaxe of wood, copper and leather. (Fitzwilliam Museum, Cambridge, E14.1950; reproduced by courtesy of the Fitzwilliam Museum, Cambridge.)

weapons was the axe. In the Old and Middle Kingdoms the conventional axe usually consisted of a semicircular copper head (see figures 23a and 24) tied to a wooden handle by cords, threaded through perforations in the copper and wrapped around lugs. At this stage there was little difference between the battleaxe and the woodworker's axe. In the Middle Kingdom, however, some battleaxes had longer blades with concave sides narrowing down to a curved edge (figure 23b). Another

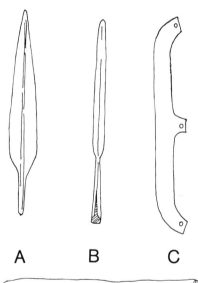

25. (Left) Development of the Egyptian spear: A, copper tanged blade (Old and Middle Kingdoms); B, copper socketed blade (New Kingdom); C, copper halberd blade (Middle and New Kingdoms).

26. (Below) Scene in a military workshop showing a craftsman checking the straightness of an arrow, from an unknown tomb at Saqqara, New Kingdom. (After Martin, 1991.)

27. (Bottom) The two major types of Egyptian bow: A, self bow; B, recurved composite bow.

A   B   C

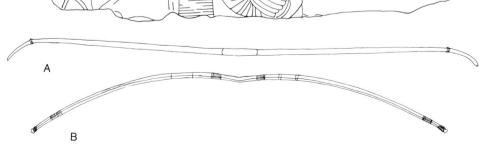

A

B

type of axe, described as 'scalloped' or 'tanged' (figure 23c), was also particularly common in the Middle Kingdom; it had a convex cutting edge and three tangs by which it was attached to the haft. Eventually, by the New Kingdom, the blade of the conventional battleaxe had been refined into a much longer, narrower and straighter form (figure 23d), designed to achieve deeper penetration. In addition, a more fragile openwork axe (figure 23e), evidently intended purely for ceremonial or funerary purposes, was introduced at the beginning of the Eighteenth Dynasty.

The Egyptian spear typically consisted of a pointed metal blade attached to a wooden shaft. In the Old and Middle Kingdoms the blade was of copper or flint and was attached to the shaft by a tang (figure 25a), but in the New Kingdom bronze blades (figure 25b), often attached by means of a socket, became more common. Whereas the conventional spear was intended to be thrown at the enemy, there was also a form of halberd (figure 25c), which was effectively a spear shaft fitted with an axe blade and used for cutting and slashing. From the Middle Kingdom onwards the dagger grew in popularity as a weapon for stabbing and crushing at close quarters. The two-edged blade, usually riveted (before the New Kingdom) to a bone or ivory handle, was sometimes decorated with grooves in the form of plants or birds.

The bow and arrow was a crucial element in Egyptian weaponry (figure 26). Along with plaited slings, bows provided a long-range assault that backed up hand-to-hand fighting with slashing and stabbing weapons. In the late Predynastic Period the 'horn bow' was in common use; this consisted of a pair of antelope horns connected by a central piece of wood (figure 18). By the Dynastic Period, archers were most commonly depicted using a 'self' (or simple) bow, firing reed arrows, fletched with three feathers and tipped with flint or hardwood (later bronze) points. The self bow (figure 27a), usually between 1 and 2 metres in length, was made up of a wooden rod, narrowing at either end, and strung with twisted gut. The longer self bows, often strengthened at certain points by binding with cord, tended to be either straighter than before or 'recurved'. The recurved bow (figure 27b), which consisted of two convex sections, had greater power and range.

The late Fifth Dynasty rock-cut tombs of the nobles Shedu and Inti, at Deshasheh in Middle Egypt, are decorated with some unusual relief scenes of warfare against Asiatics, including (in the tomb of Inti, figure 28) a depiction of a group of Egyptian soldiers attacking a Palestinian fortress. The kilted Egyptian soldiers are engaged in hand-to-hand combat using spears and axes, while some of the defending Asiatics are shown pierced with arrows, indicating that the footsoldiers' advance was backed up by a hail of arrows from Egyptian archers. A scaling

28.   Scene of siege warfare from the tomb of Inti at Deshasheh, showing a group of soldiers using a scaling ladder to capture a Palestinian fortress, Fifth Dynasty.

29.   Scene showing soldiers using a mobile siege tower, from the tomb of the general Intef at Thebes, Eleventh Dynasty.

ladder is shown propped up against the battlements and at the base of the fortress a group of soldiers are evidently attempting to undermine the wall. A wall painting in the Sixth Dynasty tomb of Kaemheset, at Saqqara, shows another scaling ladder propped against a city wall — this ladder is furnished with wheels at the base.

About two hundred years later, as evidenced in another group of provincial governors' tombs, at Beni Hasan, scenes of siege warfare had become common elements in Middle Kingdom wall paintings, probably harking back to the more anarchic times of the First Intermediate Period. A scene in the tomb of the Eleventh Dynasty noble Khety shows a pair of Middle Kingdom soldiers, apparently under the protection of a mobile roofed structure, advancing towards a fortress with a long pole — perhaps an early battering ram — thrust out in front of them. The Theban tomb of Intef, an Eleventh Dynasty general, contained a depiction of a type of mobile siege tower (figure 29). Apart from these refinements, however, the weaponry being used by the Egyptians and their opponents — a combination of bows and arrows, shields, spears and axes — remained virtually unchanged from the Sixth to Thirteenth Dynasties. It was not until the end of the Middle Kingdom that Egypt received an abrupt lesson in the dangers of military complacency, when the throne was seized by the Hyksos Dynasties, a group of Asiatic kings ruling from power bases in the Delta.

Technological innovation in the New Kingdom

Egypt's temporary domination by the Hyksos was an unequivocal warning of the dangers of allowing the political and military initiative to pass to the Asiatics. When the Theban princes Kamose and his son Ahmose eventually succeeded in defeating the Hyksos, two things must have been abundantly clear: Egypt would have to expand into Syria-Palestine, in order to provide a buffer zone protecting its vulnerable north-eastern border, and the traditional weaponry of the Egyptian army would need to be radically modernised to keep pace with the military innovations of their neighbours.

Among the most crucial innovations was the introduction of the horse-drawn chariot (Egyptian *wrrt* or *mrkbt*). The typical Egyptian chariot consisted of a light wooden semicircular framework with an open back, surmounting an axle and two wheels of four or six spokes (figure 30). The wheels, usually about a metre in diameter, were meticulously assembled from small pieces of wood and bound together with leather tyres. Two horses were yoked to the chassis by a long pole attached to the centre of the axle. The deployment of highly mobile chariots, each manned by a driver and a warrior (armed with spear, shield and bow), provided a more intense and precise means of raining arrows on the

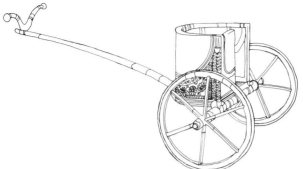

30. The horse-drawn chariot, introduced into Egypt during the Second Intermediate Period.

opposition as well as allowing the routed enemy to be pursued and dispatched more effectively (figure 31). The chariot is often depicted in reliefs and paintings (figure 32) but only eleven examples have survived, including four from the tomb of Tutankhamun (Cairo, Egyptian Museum), which were found in a dismantled state but have now been reconstructed.

According to the autobiographical inscription of King Ahmose's admiral, Ahmose son of Ibana, in his tomb at el-Kab, the Egyptian army that defeated the Hyksos was already using the chariot. Ahmose, who also fought in the armies of Amenophis I and Tuthmosis I, writes: 'I followed the king [Ahmose] on foot when he was riding around in his chariot. When the city of Avaris was under siege, I fought bravely in his majesty's presence.'

31. Two soldiers in a chariot, New Kingdom. (After Littauer.)

32. Scene of Seti I fighting in a chariot, on an external wall of the great hypostyle hall at Karnak Temple, New Kingdom. (Photograph: Ian Shaw.)

Apart from its value as a piece of military technology, the chariot was of paramount social and political significance since it heralded the appearance of the chariot corps: a new aristocratic warrior class modelled on the ubiquitous Asiatic military elite known to the Egyptians as the *maryannu* ('young heroes'). The depiction of the triumphant New Kingdom pharaoh as a charioteer (figure 32) shows that the chariot was quickly absorbed into the royal regalia, becoming as powerful a symbol of domination as the Predynastic mace. The royal chariot itself was treated as a heroic personality with gods overseeing each of its named components.

The problems of maintaining a chariot in good order are indicated by a late Nineteenth Dynasty papyrus in the British Museum (Papyrus Anastasi I; EA 10247, figure 33). This described the adventures of an Egyptian charioteer in Canaan, including his visit to a chariot repair shop in Joppa:

'You are brought into the armoury and workshops surround you — you do all that you have wished. They take care of your chariot so that it is no longer loose. Your pole is freshly trimmed and its attachments are fitted on. They put bindings on your collar piece ... and they fix up your yoke. They apply your ensign, engraved with a chisel, and they put a handle on your whip and attach a lash to it. You sally forth quickly to fight at the pass and accomplish glorious deeds.'

The New Kingdom army was also strengthened by various innovations in the equipment of the footsoldier. Body armour, in the form of small bronze plates riveted to linen or leather jerkins, was introduced by the early New Kingdom, and a smaller type of shield, with a tapered lower half, began to be used. The use of helmets remained rare among native Egyptian soldiers, although a new type of headgear was introduced into the royal regalia: a war helmet made of leather sewn with metal discs, usually described as the war (or blue) crown (figure 34).

The use of a new technique of gluing strips of horn and sinew to a wooden self bow produced the more elastic composite bow, with a considerably greater range than before. There were two types of composite bow: recurved and triangular. A new form of dagger, with the

33. Papyrus Anastasi I, a hieratic text describing a visit to a chariot repair shop. New Kingdom. (British Museum, EA 10247; reproduced by courtesy of the Trustees of the British Museum.)

34. Relief fragment showing Ramesses II wearing the blue 'war' crown, probably from Tanis, New Kingdom.

narrow blade and tang cast all in one, appeared at the beginning of the New Kingdom and gradually developed into a weapon resembling a short sword. The most specialised form of dagger was the *khepesh*, a scimitar-like weapon with a curved blade modelled on an Asiatic form that first appeared in the Second Intermediate Period. The northern exterior wall of the mortuary temple of Ramesses III (Medinet Habu) is decorated with episodes from the war against the Sea Peoples (*c*.1164 BC), including a scene of the official allocation of various types of arms (spears, helmets, bows, quivers, *khepesh* daggers and shields) to the soldiers.

Among the foreign mercenaries introduced into the Egyptian army in the late New Kingdom were Libyans, often shown with feathers on their heads and armed with bows, and Syrians armed with spears and *khepesh* daggers. But perhaps the most distinctive, in terms of arms and armour, were the Sherden, one of the groups described as Sea Peoples (see chapter 7). The origins of the Sherden probably lay in northern Syria but as far as the Egyptian records are concerned they first appeared as part of Ramesses II's army in his campaigns against the Hittites. In contrast to the native Egyptian soldiers, who appear to have

35. Scene showing Sherden mercenaries at the battle of Qadesh, from the Great Temple at Abu Simbel, Nineteenth Dynasty. (Photograph: Ian Shaw.)

served primarily as archers, the Sherden fought with sword and spear. They are instantly recognisable by their unusual headgear, a round leather helmet (sometimes with cheek protectors) surmounted by a pair of curving horns on either side of a spike, which is itself topped by a sphere or disc (figures 35 and 47). They also carry a round shield and wear a distinctive kilt, longer at the back than the front. The long tapering sword with which they are often armed is not specific to the Sherden but a lengthened form of a common type of dagger used throughout the Levant during the Middle Bronze Age.

In one of Ramesses II's earlier campaigns in Syria-Palestine a group of foreign mercenaries, wearing tasselled kilts and carrying round shields decorated with bosses, are shown storming the fortress of Deper in Amurru; their horned helmets (unusually shown in profile) suggest that they may have been Sherden, although no spike or disc is shown in the centre of the helmet. In Merneptah's first Libyan war (*c.*1207 BC) the Sherden appear as allies of the Libyans, fighting against the Egyptians, although they are distinguishable from the Egyptianised Sherden by the fact that their helmets were shaped to the backs of their necks and, like the unnamed mercenaries at Deper, there was no disc shape between the horns.

6
Imperial strategies
and international diplomacy

The Egyptian empire

The Egyptian 'empire' in Western Asia lasted perhaps as long as eight hundred years, but throughout this period the various sources of evidence are often difficult to reconcile. The essential dilemma is encountered in assimilating the contemporary Egyptian descriptions of military campaigns and victories, which fall mostly within the realm of propaganda and bravado, with the more patchily surviving evidence of more delicate diplomatic activity. If it were not for the survival of a set of cuneiform letters between Egyptian and Western Asiatic rulers, found at Amarna in 1887-92, the study of the Egyptian empire in Western Asia would be dominated far more by the language of warfare than by that of diplomacy.

In the rest of the ancient Near East there was a strong tradition of treaties, by which power blocks were built up and maintained. There were two basic types of treaty in the second millennium BC, distinguished by the Akkadian terms *riksu* (a parity treaty) and *ade* (essentially an oath of loyalty or vassal treaty). In Syria-Palestine these kinds of texts seem to have appeared at a particularly early date, probably a natural consequence of the profusion of local princes in the Levant who were constantly obliged to clarify their positions by means of vassal and parity relationships. It was inevitable that Egypt should eventually bolster its domination of the region by assuming a pre-eminent role in this diplomatic activity. The use of Akkadian and Babylonian dialects as the *lingua franca* of treaties and correspondence, however, suggests that Egypt was simply absorbed into an existing network of international diplomacy, the origins of which probably lay in Mesopotamia.

Throughout the Old and Middle Kingdoms southern Syria-Palestine (figure 36) was regarded as part of the Egyptian sphere of influence, but it was not until the reign of the Twelfth Dynasty ruler Sesostris III (ruled 1878-1841 BC) that Egypt began to play the part of a true international power. With a new northern capital aggressively named Itj-tawy ('Seizing the Two Lands') established by Amenemhat I in the area of Lisht, the scene was set for a more vigorous foreign policy both in Nubia and in Syria-Palestine. Regular envoys were sent to such Syrian city-states as Ugarit and Byblos, and there was an increase both in foreign trade and in the fortification of Egypt's north-eastern frontier. The growing Egyptian influence on Syria-Palestine in the Middle Kingdom is indicated by the fact that the native rulers of Byblos were writ-

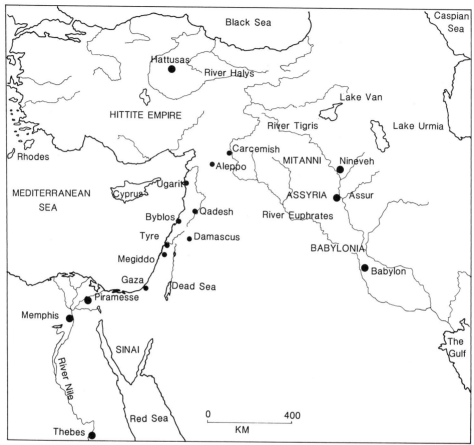

36. Map of Egypt, the Levant and Western Asia during the New Kingdom.

ing their names in Egyptian hieroglyphs and using the Egyptian title of *ḥaty-ʿ* (provincial governor).

Sesostris III was primarily concerned with the subjugation of Nubia, but he seems to have fought one campaign in Retennu (the Egyptian term for Syria-Palestine), culminating in the capture of the city of Shechem. This incident is recorded in the stele from the tomb of a military official of Sesostris III called Khusobek at Abydos. Khusobek captured a prisoner in the battle at Shechem and was personally rewarded by the king with 'a staff of electrum, a bow and a dagger wrought with electrum, together with his [the prisoner's] weapons'. There is also a roughly contemporary stele found at the village of Mit Rahina (on the site of Memphis), which mentions booty from 'Asia'. In general, however, the Middle Kingdom pharaohs pursued a relatively naive policy in the Levant, the ultimate consequence of which was to be infiltration by the 'rulers of foreign lands' and the ensuing humiliation of the Second Intermediate Period.

The Eighteenth Dynasty rulers adopted a more mature approach to international relations. As early as the reign of Ahmose (ruled 1570-1546 BC) they were laying the foundations of their Asiatic empire by campaigning in southern Retennu, but the crucial difference from their earlier forays into the Levant was the increasing use of diplomacy. The rapid construction of a framework of alliances and treaties took place alongside the adoption of Asiatic weaponry and methods of warfare.

The battle of Megiddo

Egypt's main rival in the first half of the Eighteenth Dynasty was Mitanni, a kingdom sandwiched between the growing powers of Hatti and Assyria (figure 36). By the time of Tuthmosis III Mitanni had established itself as the dominant influence on the city-states of Syria. During the reign of Tuthmosis III's stepmother Hatshepsut there had apparently been no Egyptian military campaigns in Western Asia, and the conquests of his grandfather, Tuthmosis I (who had placed a boundary stele as far north as the bank of the Euphrates), were being rapidly whittled away.

In about 1503 BC, less than a year after he came to the throne, Tuthmosis III embarked on his first, and perhaps most significant, expedition in order to thwart a 'revolt' of city-states led by the prince of Qadesh and doubtless backed by Mitanni. He marched his army from the eastern Nile Delta, via Gaza and Yemma, to the plain of Esdraelon (figure 37), leaving his general Djehuty to lay siege to the town of Joppa (modern Jaffa). According to a legend preserved on the Rammeside Papyrus Harris 500 at the British Museum, Djehuty's men, like Ali Baba, were smuggled into Joppa inside baskets. Whatever the truth of this story, Djehuty himself was a historical character and his tomb at Thebes contains an inscription describing his role in the campaign.

When Tuthmosis III arrived at Yemma he was informed that the enemy were waiting for him on the far side of the Carmel ridge, using the city of Megiddo (the Biblical Armageddon) as their base. A council of war then took place between the king and his generals: this is probably more of a literary device than a record of a real event, providing the narrator of the *Annals* with an opportunity to demonstrate the king's bravery and tactical abilities. There appear to have been three possible strategies: to follow the most direct route across the ridge, emerging about 1.5 km (1 mile) from Megiddo; to take the path northwards to the town of Djefty, emerging to the west of Megiddo; or to take the more southerly route via the town of Taanach, about 8 km (5 miles) south-east of Megiddo. The king chose the most dangerous approach — the direct route — which would take the army through a narrow pass, forcing them to march slowly one after the other, relying solely on the element of surprise.

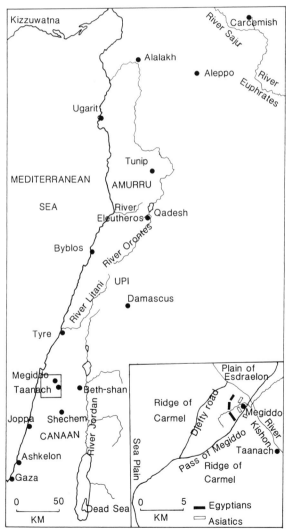

37. Map of the Levant in the Eighteenth Dynasty, with inset showing the route taken by Tuthmosis III in his final approach to the battle of Megiddo.

The journey across the Carmel range took three days, ending with a lengthy but safe passage through the narrow defile. The army then descended on to the plain and immediately found itself within a few hundred metres of the confederation of Asiatic troops encamped for the night in front of the city of Megiddo. The following morning Tuthmosis III's troops launched a frontal attack that routed the enemy, described as 'millions of men, hundreds of thousands of the greatest of all lands, standing in their chariots'. In their haste to take shelter in Megiddo, the fleeing troops were said to have accidentally locked out the kings of Qadesh and Megiddo, who had to be dragged on to the battlements by their clothing. After a seven-month siege the city was captured, bringing the campaign to a successful conclusion. The victory at Megiddo was the culmination of the first of seventeen campaigns undertaken by Tuthmosis III, which are chronicled in the *Annals* of his reign, compiled by the military scribe Tjaneni and inscribed on the walls of the Hall of Annals in the Temple of Amun-Re at Karnak.

Tuthmosis III backed up his military achievements in Retennu with the creation of a network of garrisons and numerous vassal treaties. In his sixth campaign he adopted a more long-term strategy, taking back 36 chiefs' sons to the Egyptian court so that they could be held as hostages, indoctrinated with Egyptian ideas and eventually restored to their thrones as puppet rulers. Egyptian officials, such as the general Djehuty, began to be appointed as viceroys in Retennu, bearing the Akkadian titles *rabisu* (overseer) and *sakinu* (resident) and probably having equal rank with the local princes. By the Amarna Period there seem to have been three such Egyptian governors in Syria-Palestine, corresponding to the administrative zones of Amurru, Upi and Canaan (figure 36). The three *rabisus* formed a court of arbitration to settle disputes between the vassal princes, and there was regular correspondence, via royal envoys, between the princes, *rabisus* and the pharaoh. Occasionally the local princes complained about the conduct of a *rabisu*, as in the letter from Ribaddi, the ruler of Byblos, protesting that Pakhura, the *rabisu* of Upi, had overstepped the mark in allocating a troop of Bedouin soldiers to the city militia.

The Amarna Letters: diplomacy in the New Kingdom

Tuthmosis III's successors had varying degrees of success in maintaining the empire. By the reign of Amenophis III — who fought only one campaign in Retennu, in the fifth year of his reign — the evolution of a strong mesh of diplomatic links seems to have allowed the emphasis to shift completely from battles to treaties. At a local level, the Egyptian garrisons in Syria-Palestine were able to police both the vassal cities and the troublesome bands of nomadic peoples such as the

Shasu and Apiru. On a wider international level, treaties were drawn up, gifts traded and royal sons and daughters given in marriage between the kings of Egypt, Mitanni, Assyria, Babylonia, Arzawa, Alashiya (Cyprus) and Hatti. It is this golden age of ancient diplomacy that is documented in the archive of 'Amarna Letters', discovered under the Bureau for the Correspondence of Pharaoh in the capital city of Akhenaten (ruled 1350-1334 BC) at Amarna, as well as caches of similar cuneiform tablets found at the sites of Alalakh, Taanach and Boghazköy.

The Amarna correspondence consists of nearly 350 small rectangular clay tablets inscribed in cuneiform script. Couched in a Babylonian dialect and a great deal of diplomatic jargon, most of the tablets are letters sent from the princes of city-states in Syria-Palestine to the king of Egypt or his representative the *rabisu*. About one-fifth of them were sent by Ribaddi of Byblos, who was once rebuked by the pharaoh for his obsession with letter writing. A whole series of Ribaddi's letters appear to have been pleas for military assistance, including this desperate plea for help:

'May it seem right to the Lord, Sun of the Lands, to give me twenty teams of horses. Send help quickly to protect Sumura town. All the remaining garrison troops are having problems and there are only a few people in this city. If you fail to send any soldiers, there will be no city left at all.'

Because the letters from vassals never include dates and rarely give the name of the sender or receiver, the problem of their correct chronological order has never been satisfactorily solved, although there are a few clues such as references to contemporary vassal princes and the use of the pet name Mayati for the princess Meretaten.

Apart from these chronological uncertainties, the historical value of the Amarna Letters is reduced by the almost total absence of letters sent by the pharaoh and the fact that the archive probably dates only to a short period of about ten years in the mid fourteenth century BC. The importance of the surviving correspondence, however, is that it conveys an impression of the unscrupulous diplomatic machinations and double-dealing during the New Kingdom, thus counterbalancing the relentless depiction of heroic victories and streams of tribute bearers presented on the walls of Egyptian temples.

A small number of the letters (two labelled with dates in hieratic script) were sent from Burnaburiash of Babylon and Tushratta of Mitanni to Amenophis III and Akhenaten (figure 38). The rulers address one another as 'brother' — as opposed to the terms 'father', 'sun' and 'god' used by vassal princes to address the pharaoh — and send such messages as congratulations on accession to the throne, announcement of

38. A cuneiform letter written by the Mitannian king, Tushratta, to Amenophis III, with an ink archival label written in hieratic, Eighteenth Dynasty. (British Museum, WA 29793; reproduced by courtesy of the Trustees of the British Museum.)

their own accession or complaints concerning the poor quality (or non-arrival) of gifts. The home territory of Egypt itself was not yet under threat from the other great powers, but the rulers of the various empires were keen to ensure that the Egyptian king did not develop too close an alliance with any of their rivals.

The battle of Qadesh

Ramesses II was the last pharaoh with realistic imperial ambitions in Syria-Palestine. Like Tuthmosis III he had grown up in an age when the northern provinces of Retennu were neglected and allowed to slip gradually out of Egyptian control. This time, however, the empire that was benefiting from Egypt's weakness was not Mitanni (now in irreversible decline) but the increasingly powerful Hittites. During the years of the Amarna Period and its aftermath it had been the Hittites who took advantage of the power vacuum in Retennu while Egypt was absorbed in its own internal struggles. According to a cuneiform tablet

39. Scene showing Egyptian chariots at the battle of Qadesh, from the temple of Ramesses II, Abydos, Nineteenth Dynasty. (Photograph: Ian Shaw.)

from the archives of the Hittite capital of Hattushash (modern Boghazköy), Suppiluliumas I, the Hittite king who had defeated King Tushratta of Mitanni and effectively usurped the pharaohs' role as the dominant power in the Levant, even received a plea from a widowed late Eighteenth Dynasty queen (perhaps Ankhsenamun, the wife of Tutankhamun) to allow her to marry a Hittite prince.

Despite an apparently resounding victory over the Hittites at Qadesh (*c*.1290 BC), Ramesses II's father, Seti I, had come to an agreement with the Hittite king Muwatallis by which Qadesh and Amurru (the northernmost province of Retennu) were retained by the Hittites, in return for the guarantee that they would not interfere with Egyptian interests in Canaan and Upi. This must have seemed a satisfactory solution at the time, but for Ramesses II, casting himself in the role of Tuthmosis III, only total control of Syria-Palestine would suffice.

In the summer of the fourth year of his reign (*c*.1275 BC) Ramesses succeeded in consolidating Egyptian control of the provinces of Canaan and Upi and recaptured Amurru without coming into direct conflict with the Hittites. He then forced Benteshina, the prince of Amurru, to sign a vassal treaty with Egypt. Since, however, the Hittites by now regarded Amurru as a legitimate part of their empire, Muwatallis immediately swore a sacred oath that he would regain the Syrian territories and crush the Egyptian king. For his part, Ramesses was now keen to capitalise on his successes by pushing forward into the area of central Syria and the city of Qadesh. The scene was therefore set, in the spring of 1274 BC, for the best documented Bronze Age conflict: the battle of Qadesh. There are at least thirteen surviving Egyptian versions of the battle, in three different forms (a Poem, Bulletin and Reliefs) recorded both on papyri and on the walls of Ramesses' temples in Egypt and Nubia (figures 35, 39 and 40).

The plan adopted by Ramesses in his second campaign was to send a particular section of his army (referred to as Na'arn) northwards via the Phoenician coast, while the main army, divided into four divisions (named Amun, Pre, Ptah and Seth), marched through Canaan and Upi, eventually approaching Qadesh from the south. Meanwhile Muwatallis had assembled an army which, according to Egyptian estimates, consisted of 2,500 chariots and 37,000 infantrymen — more than double the size of the Egyptian forces. Morale, however, was evidently high in Ramesses' army and it marched untroubled through the newly pacified southern territories of Retennu. After a journey of about a month the

40. Scene of an Asiatic fortress being stormed, from Karnak Temple, Nineteenth Dynasty. (Photograph: Ian Shaw.)

41. Plan of the
battle of Qadesh.

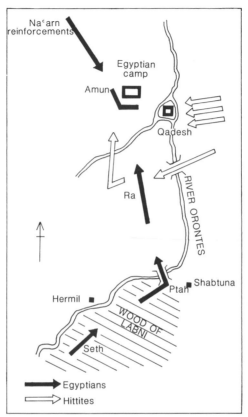

main Egyptian army was passing through the Wood of Labni, just a
short distance to the south of Qadesh, and preparing to ford the river
Orontes. At this point they captured two Shasu Bedouin, who con-
vinced them that the Hittites were still far away to the north in the
region of Aleppo. Ramesses therefore marched on ahead with the first
division, Amun, and began to set up camp near Qadesh, planning to lay
siege to it the following day.

It soon emerged, through the capture of two Hittite spies, that
Muwatallis and his army were already encamped nearby, just on the
other side of Qadesh, and ready to attack. Unfortunately, however, the
Pre division of the Egyptian army was still on its way from the river
Orontes to the new camp, while the two other divisions were still in the
Wood of Labni. Before anything could be done to remedy this situation

42. Egypto-Hittite peace treaty, from Karnak Temple, Nineteenth Dynasty. (Reproduced by courtesy of Kenneth Kitchen.)

43. Hittite 'marriage stele', from Abu Simbel, New Kingdom. (Photograph: Ian Shaw.)

the Hittite chariots launched their attack, taking the Pre division by surprise and sending them fleeing north towards the Egyptian camp (figure 41). It was then that Ramesses is supposed to have valiantly rallied the combined troops of Amun and Pre in an attempt to rescue the situation. Although he is quoted as saying 'Hold your ground and steady yourself my shield bearer! I will attack them like the swoop of the falcon, killing, slaughtering and casting them to the ground', it is clear that the Egyptians and their king might have been totally overwhelmed at this stage if it had not been for the timely arrival of the Na'arn troops, who had come by the coastal route and marched eastwards to Qadesh. With the aid of the Na'arn, the Amun and Pre divisions were able to regroup and push back the Hittite chariotry, thus affording valuable breathing space so that the Ptah and Seth divisions could catch up with the rest.

The next stage of the conflict took place the following morning, as the two armies faced each other on either side of the Orontes. The Hittites still had the numerical advantage but they had probably suffered heavy losses in their chariotry. Ramesses kept the initiative by launching an attack across the river; this was at first victorious but eventually, through sheer weight of numbers, a situation of stalemate set in. In the subsequent exchange of envoys an uneasy peace was made, allowing each party to claim some degree of success. Ramesses, however, refused to make a treaty as his father had done and he returned to Egypt with the control of Amurru still unresolved. Moreover, as soon as he had retreated the Hittites not only regained control of Amurru, sending prince Benteshina into exile, but also pushed down into Upi, thus once more reducing the Egyptian empire to the borders of the province of Canaan.

Although Ramesses II clearly regarded the battle of Qadesh as the peak of his entire reign, there can be little doubt that it was the last flourish of the Egyptian empire. In about 1259 BC he was finally obliged to make a treaty with a new Hittite king, Hattusilis III, so that Egypt and Hatti could together face a growing threat from the Assyrian empire of Shalmaneser I (ruled 1273-1244 BC). The treaty was recorded on silver tablets in cuneiform and hieroglyphs, copies of which have survived in the form of a stele at Karnak Temple and a clay tablet in the Boghazköy archives (figure 42). The new links with Hatti were celebrated by marriages between Ramesses and various Hittite princesses (figure 43), just as Amenophis III had cemented the alliance with Mitanni by marrying the princesses Tadukhipa and Gilukhipa. For the rest of the Ramesside Period the control of the Levant was a matter more for envoys than soldiers.

44. Early Nile boat painted on a pottery vessel, late Predynastic (Naqada II) Period. (British Museum, EA 35324; reproduced by courtesy of the Trustees of the British Museum.)

7
Naval battles

The Nile was always the principal means of transport in Egypt, and the sailing and construction of boats can be traced back to the papyrus rafts of the Predynastic Period. Boats were commonly depicted in red paint on the buff-coloured pottery of the Naqada II Period (figure 44). The carved relief decoration on a Naqada II ivory knife handle from Gebel el-Arak (Louvre, figure 45) is the earliest Egyptian depiction of a naval battle. It shows boats with high, straight prows and sterns, usually interpreted as foreign vessels.

The early Nile boats seem to have been primarily used for the transportation of troops up and down the Nile (figure 46), but the reliefs in the Fifth Dynasty mortuary temple of King Sahure at Abusir depict a sea-borne fleet that is said to have transported his army to Syria. In the Sixth Dynasty, the official Weni is said to have taken troops to Palestine in vessels described as *nmiw* ('travelling-ships'). Most Egyptian boats, however, were unsuitable for sailing in the Mediterranean or the Red Sea: the impetus for seaborne trade therefore seems to have come from the Levantine seaboard, probably in the region of Byblos. Certainly there was a strong connection in Egyptian minds between Byblos and naval activity, since the most common word for an Egyptian sea-going vessel was *kbnt*, literally 'Byblos-boat'. It is not clear, however, whether the use of the term denotes Byblos' importance as a centre for boatbuilding, its role as a source of timber or its familiarity as a regular destination of merchant vessels. All three explanations are equally likely.

Even the sea-going boats used by the Egyptians and their neighbours were relatively simple, consisting of a rectangular sail and one or two rudder oars. When there was no following wind, tacking was not possible and the boats had to be propelled by rowers. However, the bronze age wrecks excavated at Cape Gelidonya and Ulu Burun (both sites in the eastern Mediterranean) indicate the crucial role played by small wooden cargo ships in the flow of goods across the Mediterranean between southern Europe and the Near East. It has been estimated that the Levantine port of Ugarit had as many as 150 boats in its navy and one of the Amarna Letters (see chapter 6 above) records a request for the king of Alashiya (Cyprus) to build ships for the Egyptian navy. In Egypt itself boatbuilding was a craft with a long tradition, of which the solar boat of the Fourth Dynasty King Khufu at Giza is a fine example. The Palermo Stone records the construction of a ship 52 metres in length during the reign of King Sneferu (ruled 2613-2589 BC) of the

45. Naval battle depicted on the Gebel el-Arak knife handle, late Predynastic Period. (Louvre.)

Third Dynasty, and in the Fifth Dynasty tomb of Ti (*c.*2450 BC) at Saqqara boatbuilders are depicted at work on a large vessel (figure 47).

For most of the Dynastic Period Mediterranean shipping was mainly commercial rather than military, but in the late New Kingdom a number of sea-borne foreign armies began to menace the Delta coastline, posing a new kind of challenge to the pharaohs. On an international level, various natural and political disasters along the northern coast of the Mediterranean appear to have precipitated widespread migrations and invasions that plunged the Mediterranean region into a dark age.

In the second year of the reign of Ramesses II (*c.*1278 BC) there was a raid by Sherden pirates, who were defeated and incorporated into the Egyptian army as an elite force of mercenaries. This was the first real indication of the threat posed by a loose confederation of sea-going Indo-European migrants, including the Ekwesh, Shekelesh, Tjeker, Weshesh, Teresh, Sherden, Lukka and Denyen, whom the Egyptians described as the Sea Peoples or simply 'northerners'. In an attempt to prevent further incursions by the northerners, Ramesses II built a row of fortresses along the north-western coastline.

In the fifth year of Merneptah's reign (*c.*1207 BC) an alliance of Tjehenu (Libyans), Meshwesh and Sea Peoples attempted to invade Egypt, again from the north-west. These armies had brought with them

46. Wooden model of a Nile boat with its mast removed for rowing downstream, Middle Kingdom. (British Museum, EA 34273; reproduced by courtesy of the Trustees of the British Museum.)

their families and possessions, suggesting that their intention was to settle rather than simply to plunder. The battle with which Merneptah eventually repelled this first wave of Sea Peoples is recorded on a wall of the temple at Karnak. The inscriptions record that six thousand of the Sea Peoples were killed and nine thousand taken prisoner. It is probably no coincidence that the same inscription records the sending of grain to the ailing Hittite empire of Tudhaliyas IV. The attacks of the Sea Peoples from the north were evidently setting off a chain reaction of invasions and population movements along the entire Levantine seaboard. Neither Egypt nor the cities of Syria-Palestine could afford to allow the Hittite empire to fall into decline, since this would eventually leave a dangerous power vacuum, allowing the Sea Peoples to sweep down through Anatolia.

Over thirty years later, in the eighth year of the reign of Ramesses III (*c.*1174 BC), a second wave of Sea Peoples arrived on the Delta border. On this occasion they were allied with the Peleset (Philistines) and their

47. Scene of boatbuilders, from the tomb of Ti at Saqqara, Fifth Dynasty.

48. Detail from the depiction of the naval battle of Ramesses III, showing one of the Sea Peoples' boats, at Medinet Habu, Twentieth Dynasty.

attack came from the north-east by both land and sea. Contemporary texts describe the Sea Peoples' advance: 'Suddenly these peoples were on the move, scattered in war. No country could withstand their arms. The Hittites, Cilicia, Carcemish, Cyprus and other lands were cut off.' The Sea Peoples' land attack seems to have been checked by a single battle in the region of the Egyptian frontier garrisons along the northern edge of the Sinai desert. In the description of this land conflict it is noticeable that, as in the reign of Merneptah, the invaders were accompanied by their families, ox-carts and livestock.

When the Sea Peoples transferred their energies to an attack by sea, Ramesses III defeated them again in a great naval battle, which was later depicted in a complex relief sculpture on the northern outer wall of his mortuary temple at Medinet Habu. The relief shows hand-to-hand fighting between five of the Sea Peoples' boats (with prows and sterns carved in the form of birds' heads, figure 48) and four of the larger Egyptian vessels (each with a lion's head at the prow, figure 49). The Egyptian boats have rows of 20-22 oarsmen on board in addition to the archers and footsoldiers, whereas the smaller number of men on board the Sea Peoples' boats must have doubled as both warriors and rowers. One of the invaders' boats has been capsized, and the surrounding water is full of their dead.

The outcome of this naval encounter — the first properly documented sea battle — was another victory for Ramesses III. But, just as the Sherden had been assimilated into the Egyptian army after their defeat by Ramesses II, so the Sea Peoples were subsequently absorbed into the rapidly declining Egyptian empire. Although Ramesses III and his immediate successors still maintained control of Canaan, the Sea Peoples (particularly Peleset and Tjeker) were allowed to settle there and the Egyptian garrison at Beth-shan came to be manned by Peleset mercenaries. This policy must have been successful in the short term, judging from an account of a Libyan attack in the eleventh year of Ramesses III's reign (*c*.1171 BC) in which the Sea Peoples are no longer mentioned as allies against Egypt. But in the long term the Egyptians' solitary sea victory was only a postponement of the inevitable and by the end of the Twentieth Dynasty Canaan had effectively passed into the hands of the Sea Peoples. It is clear from the account of the ill fated royal trading mission of Wenamun that, by the time of King Herihor (*c*.1075 BC), the Egyptian navy was unable even to maintain regular supplies of cedarwood from Byblos.

In the seventh century BC the commercially astute Twenty-sixth Dynasty kings, based at the city of Sais in the Delta, established a large fleet of Graeco-Phoenician style war-galleys, enabling Egypt temporarily to regain control of the Levantine sea trade. But Egypt's declining military power was still primarily land-based and, although Egyptian shipwrights are documented in Babylon in the early sixth century BC, the Late Period fleet was evidently manned primarily by Phoenicians.

49. Detail from the depiction of the naval battle of Ramesses III, showing an Egyptian boat, at Medinet Habu, Twentieth Dynasty.

50. 'Victory stele' of Piye from Gebel Barkal, Late Period. (Reproduced by courtesy of Peter Clayton.)

8
Military decline

The campaigns against the Sea Peoples were clear omens of the future military fate of the Egyptians. With the onset of economic and political decline, the last battles of the native Egyptian pharaohs were desperate defensive struggles, far removed from the empire building of Sesostris III, Tuthmosis III and Ramesses II in the Middle and New Kingdoms. Many of the military actions of the Third Intermediate Period and Late Period took place on Egyptian soil, as successive waves of foreigners capitalised on the weakness of their old enemy. As with any such decline, it is difficult to pinpoint the precise causes of this new vulnerability. In the economic sphere, Egypt had become less self-sufficient in metals (particularly with the increasing importance of iron, all of which had to be imported), producing a dangerous dependence on trade with Western Asia just at the time when Egyptian influence in the Levant was at its lowest ebb. In the purely military sphere there is growing evidence that native Egyptians were once more gravitating towards the traditional religious and bureaucratic routes to power, leaving the Egyptian army dangerously dominated by foreign mercenaries and immigrants.

Eventually the campaigning of the Kushite (Twenty-fifth Dynasty) pharaohs in Syria-Palestine led to direct conflict with a new imperial power: the Assyrians. In 674 BC Taharqa (ruled 690-664 BC) was able temporarily to deter the invading forces of the Assyrian king Esarhaddon (ruled 680-669 BC), but in the ensuing decade the Assyrians made repeated successful incursions into the heart of Egypt, and only the periodic rebellions of the Medes and Scythians — at the other end of the Assyrian empire — prevented them from gaining a more permanent grip on the Nile valley. In 671 BC Esarhaddon captured Memphis, describing the event with relish in an inscription at Senjirli:

'I laid siege to Memphis, Taharqa's royal residence, and conquered it in half a day by means of mines, breaches and assault ladders; I destroyed it, tore down its walls and burnt it down. His 'queen', the women of his palace, Ushanahuru, his heir apparent, his other children, his possessions, horses, large and small cattle beyond counting, I carried away as booty to Assyria. All Ethiopians I deported from Egypt — leaving not even one to do homage to me. Everywhere in Egypt, I appointed new local kings, governors, officers (*saknu*), harbour overseers, officials and administration personnel' (Pritchard, 1969: 293).

Three years later Taharqa had succeeded in briefly reasserting the

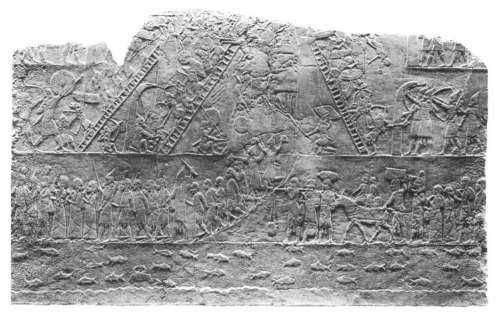

51. Fragment of Assyrian relief from the palace of Ashurbanipal at Nineveh, showing the storming of an Egyptian town, *c*.645 BC. (British Museum, WA 124928; reproduced by courtesy of the Trustees of the British Museum.)

Kushite hegemony over Egypt, while the Assyrians were distracted by problems elsewhere. But by 667 BC Esarhaddon's successor Ashurbanipal (ruled 668-627 BC) had penetrated beyond the Delta into Upper Egypt, where he must have severely damaged morale by pillaging Thebes, the spiritual home of the Egyptians.

A fascinating insight into the campaigns of Esarhaddon and Ashurbanipal in Egypt has been provided by the survival of a fragment of relief from Ashurbanipal's palace at Nineveh (now in the British Museum; figure 51) which shows the Assyrian army laying siege to an Egyptian city. The details of this scene, such as the depiction of an Assyrian soldier undermining the city walls and others climbing ladders to the battlements, bear strong similarities with Egyptian siege representations described above (see figures 9, 28, 29 and 40), showing that ancient siege warfare from North Africa to Mesopotamia used similar tactics and weaponry. The rows of captive soldiers being marched out of the city appear to be mainly foreign mercenaries. In the bottom right-hand corner of the scene a group of native Egyptian civilians are shown clustered together with their children and possessions. The inscriptions of both Esarhaddon and Ashurbanipal show that the usual Assyrian practice of deportation was employed, with Egyptian physicians, diviners, singers, bakers, clerks and scribes (as well as prisoners of war and members of the ruling families) being resettled in the Assyrian heartland.

During the period of 340 years from the first Assyrian conquest until the arrival of Alexander the Great in 332 BC, the military history of Egypt was characterised by a complicated succession of peaks and troughs. Just as the Egyptians had cynically played off the princes of the Levant against one another, the Assyrians maintained their control over Egypt by supporting a number of local rulers. The princes of the Delta, particularly Necho I of Sais, effectively became vassals of the Assyrian regime, shored up in order to prevent a resurgence of the Kushite dynasty.

When the Assyrian empire itself began to go into a decline in the mid seventh century BC it was the Saite king Psammetichus I (ruled 664-610 BC), the son of Necho I, who was able to take advantage of the sudden political vacuum. He united Egypt under the rule of the Twenty-sixth Dynasty, and by the end of his reign he had built up a formidable army that was significantly strengthened by the inclusion of Ionian, Carian and Phoenician mercenaries. During the reigns of his successors Necho II and Psammetichus II there were military victories in both Syria-Palestine and Nubia, but this brief re-emergence of Egypt as a world power was totally eclipsed by the rise of the Persians in the late sixth century.

During the Late Period the Egyptians found that they themselves were not exempt from the recurrent cycle of conquest, pillage, vassaldom and rebellion that had for so long been endemic in the Levant. Once they had been defeated by the Assyrians, their status was effectively reduced to that of the Syro-Palestinian princedoms, and the myth of Egyptian military supremacy could no longer be sustained.

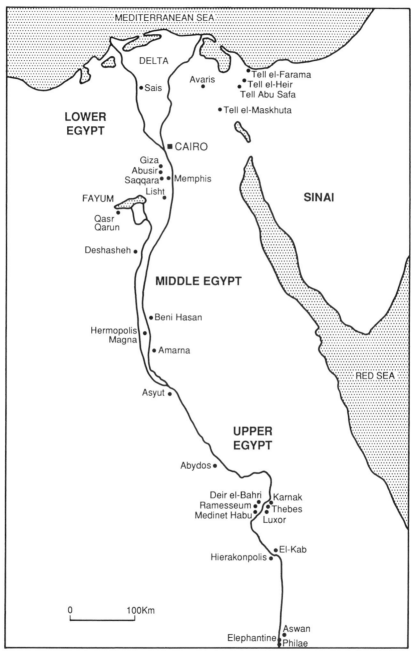

MEDITERRANEAN SEA

DELTA

• Sais

Avaris •

• Tell el-Farama
• Tell el-Heir
Tell Abu Safa

• Tell el-Maskhuta

LOWER
EGYPT

■ CAIRO

Giza •
Abusir •
Saqqara • • Memphis
• Lisht

FAYUM

Qasr •
Qarun

SINAI

Deshasheh •

MIDDLE EGYPT

• Beni Hasan

Hermopolis •
Magna

• Amarna

RED SEA

Asyut •

UPPER
EGYPT

Abydos •

Deir el-Bahri •   • Karnak
Ramesseum • • • Thebes
Medinet Habu • • Luxor

• El-Kab
Hierakonpolis •

0   100Km

Aswan
Elephantine • • Philae

52. Map of Egypt showing the location of sites mentioned in the text. (Drawn by Robert Dizon.)

9
Museums

The following museums have collections of ancient Egyptian artefacts, including weapons and other evidence of warfare. Intending visitors are advised to find out opening times before making a special journey.

United Kingdom

Ashmolean Museum of Art and Archaeology, Beaumont Street, Oxford OX1 2PH. Telephone: 0865 278000.

Birmingham Museum and Art Gallery, Chamberlain Square, Birmingham, West Midlands B3 3DH. Telephone: 021-235 2834.

Bolton Museum and Art Gallery, Le Mans Crescent, Bolton, Lancashire BL1 1SE. Telephone: 0204 22311 extension 2191.

The British Museum, Great Russell Street, London WC1B 3DG. Telephone: 071-636 1555.

Fitzwilliam Museum, Trumpington Street, Cambridge CB2 1RB. Telephone: 0223 332900.

The Manchester Museum, University of Manchester, Oxford Road, Manchester M13 9PL. Telephone: 061-275 2634.

The Petrie Museum of Egyptian Archaeology, University College London, Gower Street, London WC1E 6BT. Telephone: 071-387 7050, extension 2884.

Royal Museum of Scotland, Chambers Street, Edinburgh EH1 1JF. Telephone: 031-225 7534.

Egypt

Egyptian Museum, Tahrir Square, Cairo.

Luxor Museum of Egyptian Art, Sharia Nahr el-Nil, Luxor.

France

Musée du Louvre, Palais du Louvre, F-75041 Paris.

Italy

Museo Egizio, Palazzo dell'Accademia delle Scienze, Via Accademia delle Scienze 6, Turin.

Museo Egizio, Vatican City, Rome.

Netherlands

Rijksmuseum van Oudheden, Rapenburg 28, 2311 EW Leiden, Zuid-Holland.

United States of America
The Brooklyn Museum, 200 Eastern Parkway, Brooklyn, New York NY
  11238.
Metropolitan Museum of Art, 5th Avenue at 82nd Street, New York NY
  10028.

10
Further reading

Adams, W. Y. *Nubia: Corridor to Africa.* Allen Lane, 1982.
Breasted, J. H. *The Battle of Kadesh: A Study in the Earliest Known
  Military Strategy.* Chicago Oriental Institute, 1903.
Campbell, E. F. *The Chronology of the Amarna Letters.* The Johns
  Hopkins Press, Baltimore, 1964.
Davies, W. V. *Catalogue of Egyptian Antiquities in the British Museum,
  VII: Tools and Weapons*, 1: *Axes.* British Museum Publications,
  1987.
Emery, W. B. *Egypt in Nubia.* Hutchinson, 1965.
Emery, W. B., Smith, H. S., and Millard, A. *The Fortress of Buhen:
  The Archaeological Report.* Egypt Exploration Society, 1979.
Faulkner, R. O. 'Egyptian Seagoing Ships', *Journal of Egyptian
  Archaeology*, 26 (1940), 3-9.
Gardiner, A. H. *The Kadesh Inscriptions of Ramesses II.* Griffith
  Institute, Oxford, 1960.
Goedicke, H. (editor). *Perspectives on the Battle of Kadesh.* Halgo,
  Baltimore, 1985.
Helck, W. *Der Einfluß der Militärführer in der 18. Ägyptischen Dynastie.*
  J. C. Hinrichs Verlag, Leipzig, 1939.
Helck, W. *Die Beziehungen Ägyptens zur Vorderasien im 3. und 2.
  Jahrtausend v. Chr.* Harrasowitz, Wiesbaden, 1971.
Kitchen, K. A. *Pharaoh Triumphant: The Life and Times of Ramesses
  II, King of Egypt.* Aris and Phillips, 1982.
Landström, B. *Ships of the Pharaohs.* Allen Lane, 1970.
Lawrence, A. W. 'Ancient Egyptian Fortifications', *Journal of Egyptian Archaeology*, 51 (1965), 69-94.
Lichtheim, M. *Ancient Egyptian Literature: A Book of Readings*, I:
  The Old and Middle Kingdoms. University of California Press, 1973.
Littauer, M. A., and Crouwel, J. H. *Wheeled Vehicles and Ridden
  Animals in the Ancient Near East.* E. J. Brill, Leiden and Cologne,
  1979.
Littauer, M. A., and Crouwel, J. H. *Chariots and Related Equipment
  from the Tomb of Tut'ankhamun.* Griffith Institute, Oxford, 1985.

McLeod, W. E. *Composite Bows from the Tomb of Tut'ankhamun.* Griffith Institute, Oxford, 1970.

McLeod, W. E. *Self Bows and Other Archery Tackle from the Tomb of Tut'ankhamun.* Griffith Institute, Oxford, 1982.

Murnane, W. J. *The Road to Kadesh: A Historical Interpretation of the Battle Reliefs of King Sety I at Karnak.* Chicago Oriental Institute, 1985.

Newby, P. H. *Warrior Pharaohs: The Rise and Fall of the Egyptian Empire.* Faber, 1980.

Petrie, W. M. F. *Tools and Weapons.* Egypt Research Account, 1917.

Pritchard, J. B. *Ancient Near Eastern Texts Relating to the Old Testament.* Princeton University Press, 1969.

Sandars, N. K. *The Sea Peoples: Warriors of the Eastern Mediterranean, 1250-1150 B.C.* Thames and Hudson, 1978.

Säve-Söderbergh, T. *The Navy of the Eighteenth Egyptian Dynasty.* Uppsala University Press, 1946.

Schulman, A. R. *Military Rank, Title and Organization in the Egyptian New Kingdom.* Münchner Ägyptischer Studien 6, Berlin, 1964.

Spalinger, A. J. *Aspects of the Military Documents of the Ancient Egyptians.* Yale University Press, 1982.

Trigger, B. *History and Settlement in Lower Nubia.* Yale University Press, 1965.

Trigger, B. *Nubia under the Pharaohs.* Thames and Hudson, 1976.

Vandersleyen, C. *Les Guerres d'Amosis Fondateur de la XVIIIe Dynastie.* Fondation Egyptologique Reine Elisabeth, Brussells, 1971.

Winlock, H. E. *The Slain Soldiers of Neb-Hepet-Re' Mentu-Hotpe.* Metropolitan Museum of Art, New York, 1945.

Yadin, Y. *The Art of Warfare in Biblical Lands.* London, 1963.

Index

Page numbers in italics refer to illustrations.